SMALL MECHANICS

BOOKS BY LORNA CROZIER

POETRY

Inside Is the Sky (1976)

Crow's Black Joy (1979)

Humans and Other Beasts (1980)

No Longer Two People (with Patrick Lane) (1981)

The Weather (1983)

The Garden Going On Without Us (1985)

Angels of Flesh, Angels of Silence (1988)

Inventing the Hawk (1992)

Everything Arrives at the Light (1995)

A Saving Grace (1996)

What the Living Won't Let Go (1999)

Apocrypha of Light (2002)

Bones in Their Wings: Ghazals (2003)

Whetstone (2005)

The Blue Hour of the Day: Selected Poems (2007)

Small Mechanics (2011)

MEMOIR

Small Beneath the Sky (2009)

ANTHOLOGIES

A Sudden Radiance (with Gary Hyland) (1987)

Breathing Fire (with Patrick Lane) (1995)

Desire in Seven Voices (2000)

Addicted: Notes from the Belly of the Beast
(with Patrick Lane) (2001)

Breathing Fire 2 (with Patrick Lane) (2004)

Best Canadian Poetry 2010 (2010)

SMALL MECHANICS

poems

LORNA CROZIER

McCLELLAND & STEWART

Library and Archives Canada Cataloguing in Publication

Crozier, Lorna, 1948–
Small mechanics / Lorna Crozier.

Poems.
Issued also in electronic format.
ISBN 978-0-7710-2329-3

I. Title.

PS8555.R72S53 2011   C811.'54   C2010-905275-7

LIBRARY OF CONGRESS CONTROL NUMBER: 2010940063

We acknowledge the financial support of the Government of Canada through the Book Publishing Industry Development Program and that of the Government of Ontario through the Ontario Media Development Corporation's Ontario Book Initiative. We further acknowledge the support of the Canada Council for the Arts and the Ontario Arts Council for our publishing program.

Typeset in Dante by M&S, Toronto
Text design by Paul Dotey
Printed and bound in Canada

This book is printed on paper that is 100% recycled, ancient-forest friendly (100% post-consumer waste).

McClelland & Stewart Ltd.
75 Sherbourne Street
Toronto, Ontario
M5A 2P9
www.mcclelland.com

1 2 3 4 5   15 14 13 12 11

This book is for Patrick, my love

I want a poet who goes outside,
who knows the small mechanics
of the clothespin and the muddy boot.

CONTENTS

SMALL MECHANICS

LAST BREATH

Not a living soul about,
except for me and the magpie. I know
if I don't keep moving, he'll pluck
the breath from my body, taste it
on his tongue before it slides
down his throat, giving him new prophecies
to speak. He's the bird Noah didn't send out,
afraid he'd carry the ark's complaints to heaven.
Tonight he scallops from the copse of willows
to the power pole, stares down at me. I match him
cry for cry, not knowing what I mean but feeling
good about it, the bird part of my brain lit up.
Coyotes, too, start their music as if the magpie's
flown in to be the guest conductor
for the length of time it takes the sun to sink.
He flips his tail, bringing up the oboes
then the high notes of the flutes. Other souls,
those I sense but cannot see,
wait among the stones along the riverbank
until they're sure the magpie is distracted,
then scentless and inedible to anyone but him,
they make their wingless foray
across the ice and running water,
mouthfuls of silence that, if not for coyotes,
the magpie would hear.

DON'T SAY IT

You admire the wild grasses
for their reticence.

When you cut across the dusk for home,
the meadow is more beautiful

for all it keeps inside.
Syllables of seeds catch in your socks

but they don't need to say,
Thank you, friend,

even if you've carried them
for miles.

THE FIRST DAY OF THE YEAR

The new writer sucks her fingers
in her crib. There is nothing
to distinguish her – like the extra toe

on Hemingway's
literary cats – from all the other
babies down the block.

She is dreaming ink
though she hasn't seen it
in this world yet

and no one knows,
least of all her parents,
she loves nothing

better than the blank
flat whiteness
of the bottom sheet

when she's laid damp
from her morning bath
upon it.

BECAUSE WE ARE MADE OF MOSTLY WATER,

every time we speak,
our words are mist, are rain,
clear rivulets chattering

over sand and gravel,
over bones laid deep
in the earth. Sometimes

our words are snow.
Cold alphabets slap the cheeks,
the sting of winter slipping

from your tongue to mine,
and everything inside us
freezes shut. We speak then

as the dead do, all
the rivers knotted with ice,
our mouths odd

with cold and urgently dry
from the effort of making
no sad sound.

TRANSPLANTED

This heart met the air. Grew in the hours
between the first body and the next
a taste for things outside it: the heat
of high intensity, wind grieving
in the poplar leaves, the smell of steam
wafting through the open window
from the hot dog vendor's cart. Often it skips

a beat – grouse explode from ditches,
a man flies through the windshield,
a face the heart once knew
weeps in the corridor that gives nothing back
but unloveliness and glare.

Like a shovel that hits the earth, then rises,
and hits the earth again, it feels its own
dull blows. Some nights it is a sail billowing
with blood, a raw fist punching.
Some nights, beneath the weight of blankets,
flesh and bones, the heart remembers. Feels those
surgical gloves close around it, and goes cold.

THE UNBORN
(for Carmen)

They don't show up that often
and when they do, it's possible
to ignore them like all the other things
that go on while you sleep.

Most hauntings occur in the garden.
A wind that is not a wind fingers the bamboo,
a blurred face, perhaps a child's, appears
below the surface of the water, a fish rising
where a mouth would be, moonlight too warm
for moonlight pouring from the throats of lilies.

They seem most at home in snow
falling out of season, thickening the asters
and sprays of phlox, gathering with cold ease
along the fir's wide branches, erasing all
the day's mistakes, the soiled, the misforgotten.

In snow's unmothering abundance
you offer them a kind of birth rite:
across the drift that stops
the gate from opening, you write
what you would call them – Heart's Sorrow,
Wind Rider, Little Bell of the Bamboo Grove.

THE SOLSTICE BIRD

It's taken the rising sun two hours
to find these hills. It will take less time
tomorrow. Few things you're sure of,
this is one: under the crusted drifts

the grass is stirring. The black-capped
chickadee cries *me, me, me,*
as you fill the feeder. Such unruly conceit,
such indifference to cold and grammar.

What is winter in you begins
to shift, begins to feel a hunger.

You hold out your hand with nothing.
The bird lands anyway, the black nibs of its feet
scratching commas on your palm,

meaning: there's no end to this,
meaning: there's always some
new detail appended to the list
even though it may not be
the half-starved thing you'd choose.

FACTS

Did you know an ant has four
olfactory organs on its antennae;
the female mouse, a clitoris? This I learned
from two poets – one famous and American,
the other a student of biology and physics.

Now anything is possible:

Did you know that grass has legs and feet?
That's why it's never still
but runs on the spot like a child in an old gymnasium.

Did you know the moon cleans itself with a tongue
rough as a cat's? It licks and licks until it disappears
then comes up new again, shiny with spittle.

Did you know the yellow butterflies that feed on cabbage
have a temper; the winds, a worrying mother?

Every dusk she stands in the airy doorway of the world
and calls them home.

LICHEN

1.

The kind of scab –
round and desiccated –
a child would pick bit by bit

feeding himself
on the rock's small wound.

2.

Embossed orange seal
stamped on the hardback cover
of the *Concise Encyclopedia of Stone*.

No one signs it out, no one opens it.

If it weren't an encyclopedia
it would be a book of poems.

3.

Patch of eczema,
an itch the rock can't scratch
though the wind's scouring pad
of grit and sleet brings some relief.

4.

Something that comes close to holy:
you must fall on your knees
to see it clearly, weather's hallelujah
turned to Braille. Like rain
it will die if brought inside.

5.

A rock's memorabilia: flawed cameo
worn down by frost and wind;
tactile photo of the crab nebula
blazed into mineral
like the bright side of a shadow
burned into a Hiroshima wall.

6.

The rock's idea of a blossom –
bloom of a cynic, unscented,
bloom of an atheist, unbidden,
bloom of a woman who's lost
everything to love

yet a Midas bee caught in amber
takes all it knows of time
to beat its wings –
once, twice – and move toward it.

7.

A lidless eye that never closes;
it has seen many changes
yet does not change. In this,
poor creature, it resembles you.

8.

Crusty bright splatter,
a birthmark rubbed for luck,
bloodied by the midwife's hands.

GIVING UP

The last of the moon is fed up.
It's given them enough light below
to do something good, enough light
to read by, to find what was bright
within them.

Let them do their work in darkness, the bad
and good of it. Let the cereus cease its shining.
Let the man betray the boy he was and never once
look up.

The moon will turn itself off tonight.

The sand that is dry will stay dry.
The coonhound and the blood
will lower their heads and make no sound.

No one will go mad tonight.
No one will ride a silver slip across the waters,
and no one, no one, no one will fall
in love.

FINDING FOUR WAYS TO CELEBRATE THE HUGE MOTHS THAT KEEP ME AWAKE BY BANGING BETWEEN THE BLIND AND WINDOW AND FALLING ON MY PILLOW

I.

Though inelegant, fat with grit and gravity,
sooty-winged and always falling, they're more
spirit than flesh; each night wearing thin
as they beat the fiery air, enraptured by
the household god-who-is-all-light.

2.

The once dull-named Townsend bat
with long floppy ears and small knobs
like tree burls above its nose,
having learned to soften its sonic clicks
so the moths won't hear, is now called,
even by scientists, whispering bat.

3.

The trap springs shut. From the mouse's mouth,
its soul flaps out, brown and bigger than you would've
   guessed.
It drags its wings up the wall to the small eternities
of twitch and quickness, heavenly half-moons of cheese.

4.

Years before madness, the young Van Gogh,
after a morning of studying charcoal,
smudged his flat thumbs on the willing
white breasts of the flour merchant's wife.

GENESIS

Not that light.
The gleam on leaf and skin,
on any moving thing.

But light
at the bottom, under
stone, under each
tread of the bear's wide paw,

earth-light under earth,
light of the burnt-out,
light under the eyelid,
under-tongued,
the fierce

unsaid, un-
redeemable light.

That light,
the dark
angel's *let there be.*

ON BACH'S CELLO SUITE NO. 2 IN D MINOR

Prelude

Lacking the violin's higher reasoning,
its closeness to the mind, the cello
without touching, knows the lower body
best, the shame and glory of the belly,
the bowels, the inner thighs,
the sweat and stain of things, holy and otherwise,
– this, the cello's music, the dark vibratos,
the pitch and muscle of their sounds.

Music Is More Precious

Music is more precious
when there's less light

to read the body by. The heart,
avid listener in its warm cave,

its hibernation half-intended.
The half rhyme of Bach with water

won't let go of me though I'm not
confusing him with Handel.

Is it because of all this rain? Today
the garden is Atlantis. The moon spills

a wash across the blue of monkshood
still in bloom. There's a wash, too,

across the eyes. Eddying through rain
Bach's Cello Suite in D Minor

could be whale song
echoing for miles across the sea floor,

calling the lost,
the ones without a mother, home.

What Music Does

At night something whispers,
Go wild to the green maple
and by morning it's gone so far
it's redder than the reddest
fox – about to spring.

Its transformation startles,
leaps inside you,
yet you see it every fall,

know it the way you know
what music does
to sadness, its deepest
listening, disturbed.

Winter Coming On

Leaves falling from the maple
make a thin, poor music,
the pond below them

a cello or, better yet,
a lute lying on its back, deep-bellied
and mute. A koi rises, the old one

we used to call golden
but his lustre is gone.
So it is with me, this dark November,

my mother three months dead.
She was my shining.

What do fish hear, I wonder,
in their watery ears? Fins and tail
play the pond's cold changes,
winter coming on.

Bach lost his mother
before his voice broke.
He sang soprano in the choir.

His father went a few months later.
You can hear it in the intervals,
that early loss. Orphaned
he threw himself into organ music,

learned the stops. Myself,
I play no strings or keys.
All is undersound and longing,
the grace notes of the garden in the rain.

If Bach Were a Bird

I am reading Wang Wei
and listening to Bach though
why they go together I cannot say,
can count on only this for sure:
the Seven Sages in the Bamboo
are chickadees, know-it-all and chatty.

They're the kind of masters
who'd hit you with a stick
if they could hold one big enough
to get your full attention.

If Bach were a bird he'd be one of them,
black-capped and quick.

A Chinese proverb says
the bird sings not because
it has an answer
but because it has a song.

Wang Wei knew this,
Bach, as well, though he might
have said it in a different way
being German, not Chinese.

The chickadees need no one's
wisdom but their own.
They have their songs
and they sing them,
and you know

though you've been told
not to look for it, you know
the answer's there.

WHAT COMES NEXT

1.

Here comes my father home from fishing;
he never owned a crewel. In a tin bucket
he carries three Lac Peletier perch
for my mother to gut and scale.

Here comes my mother with a scraping
knife. She didn't know how to filet then.
At supper, the fish fried in butter,
she fingers through my portion for the thin
white slivers that could catch my breath.
No one's ever loved me better.

Here comes the silence, Sunday's
cutlery and the formal courtesy
of passing salt and butter, the only question
that gets asked, *Do you want more tea?*
my father's hand shaking as it guides
the spoon from the sugar bowl to his cup.

2.

Here comes the cold unwanted.
In the prairie dark I'm walking home
from school where my third-grade teacher
has put me in the back and told me
not to sing. I don't tell anyone;
I have no music in me.

Here comes the snow,
crystals blooming on my scarf

where my voice is coming out,
my brows and lashes feathered, my lungs
marvellous machines that manufacture
frost from breath and cold.

3.
Here come the dead. They've had enough of
mouthing words below the clouds,
enough of never asking. Straight from the heart
where there's little left of them
they start singing while we sleep.
All the windows in our house gleam white as bone.

TURNING ON THE LIGHT

The small white house, empty,
unnoticed for so long, comes back
into its own – sudden – startling to the eye –
as if it's been away and just now steps
from the darkness of the trees
to settle at the edge of the field.

By its broken gate, again and again,
a grey cat catches a grey mouse
and lets it go. No perversity or pain,
they have something to atone for.
Inside the walls, flies awake from slumber.
They pepper the wallpaper, the plates,
the facecloth stiff on a nail by the sink.
So many climb the string, they turn on the light.

A woman in the farmhouse across the field
looks out her kitchen window. For the first time
in years, she wonders where she is;
in what should be the ordinary after-supper dark,
the white house casts its glow.
The boy and girl who have never stopped
their lovemaking in the shelter of its trees
feel its light upon them and grow old.

MY FATHER, RIDING

My father's out riding in a field at dusk;
on a grey horse called Tony he moves
toward my mother's house. She is crossing
the stubble in her older sister's shoes,
holding the hem of her dress above the dust.

This is long before I am born, but I have spread
a blanket where the wild grass meets
the furrows. My father's favourite things
sit upon it, white chicken on white bread,
a Pilsner Old-Fashioned, a wedge of rhubarb pie.
How close they are to meeting!

The horse smells her now. It flicks its ears
at the rustle of her dress against her legs,
the crackle of her borrowed shoes on stubble.
Does the rider see her? He looks right through me.
For her, he is on a grey horse soon beside her,
and he's reaching down. For me, he slides
to the ground, sits on the blanket, and tips his beer.
I can feel its coolness in his mouth.

ANGEL OF GRIEF

He shows up in my mother's bedroom,
wings soiled, all down the sides
piss-yellow stains, the rust of blood,
and along the feathers' edge a dazzling green
as if to get to me, he flew too low across the sea
and gathered up its phosphorescence.

Part of me understands why he is here.
I've grief enough. And there's something
sacred about this place and what I'm doing,
emptying my mother's dresser,
the only thing she claimed as hers alone,
the house too small, too poor to keep a secret.

She warned me as a child not to snoop
but I find nothing in the drawers a daughter
shouldn't see: two swimsuits, homemade,
loosening around the legs, white cotton bras
and briefs she ordered from the catalogue,
a few with bare elastic showing, all intimate
and washed and washed – I couldn't be sadder.

The angel doesn't speak, at least not here,
not to me, but there's a susurration
in the room as if he's brought the wind with him
to keep alive his wings. He won't be trapped.
I don't know if he is weeping. His head is bowed,
white hair falling over ears and brow
– enough of him. Here, he's less
important than my mother, her last things;

they slip through my fingers into the garbage sack
and leave their mark on me like scalding water.

ANGEL OF LONELINESS

Of course there's no one,
especially not an angel
though the air seems overly receptive
as if it's leaving room for something
to arrive. The only tracks in the snow
are her own, leading from the back door
to the birdfeeder where wind above the drifts
fashions wings of such a force and size
she can feel the muscles
underneath the pinions as they push her back
and sweep across the yard.

There's no one here
but her, a lone woman breaking
a path to the feeder, her body
all these years untouched,
unfeathered. It's the cold –
this winter there's too much of it –
that makes its presence known,
inside and out. She can feel it
blunt her skin, grip the morning
and all that's tethered to the earth
in its boneless fist.

NIGHT WALK

Cautious on ice, after supper I walk the town,
the sideroads slick, in some spots you have to
put your foot down flat like a block of wood
and move stiff-legged. I worry about a fall,
a broken hip, old bone that may not mend.

The moon knows I'm the only one about.
Dusted with snow, its light is feeble, just
enough to keep me going. It's early evening;
emptiness has found a way to show itself,
along the street the houses small and dark.
The moon's so tired of metaphor, it wants
no more of human longing.

Where there are trees, three in a row at least,
the ice has melted underfoot. The woody roots
electric, send out their heat.
Are trees what warm us, unbeknown,
when the world is hard and cold?

Alone on Main Street I lower my hood
and listen. Coyotes are talking to themselves
in the nearby hills, their calls joyous, obstreperous,
beautifully by us un-understood.

Once, twice, a truck goes past.
I raise my hand to wave but I can't see
if anyone is waving back.

THE HOUR OF SNOW

   Everything quiets, everything
moves hesitant and slow, even
the feisty pup flops down, his head
between his paws, and in his dream
there's no running after anything.

Outside, the fields pull cold and brightness
over them, those wind-washed sheets.
Time to consider snow's sophistry,
its mortar and mend,
before the fields resume their job,
laying down the path to heaven.

You walk into your breath – small
frosted cloud in front of you –
and breathe it in,
brief memento of who you were
a heartbeat past. Snow gives you
this hour to say goodbye to everything,
your hair, the thick and thin of it,
gone white with grief.

MERCY

The old god drops his flesh and bones
and rushes down as wind and nothing else,
not word or light or mercy. It batters the town,
slams a sheet of plywood against the curling rink,
shoves me down the alley in my slippery shoes.
In the third yard down, on a metal clothesline pole,
strung by their necks with ropes, two coyotes sway,
weight and counterweight in a faceless clock.
Beauty graces them, even now, death graces them.
Is it a curse to love the world too much,
to praise its paws and hooves,
its thick-furred creatures, each life a fear in me?
The wind saves nothing on this earth.
The coyotes hang like coyotes from an ugly tree.
Their throats don't make a sound.

GETTING USED TO IT

Our lovemaking that day was slow and tender
as if both our childhoods crowded around our bed.
My mother, on her own now sixteen years,
had phoned. Her brother's widow two doors down
was having family over, but not her. "It's okay,"
Mom said. "I'm used to being treated this way,"
then, "Happy New Year," her loneliness
a hard salt on my skin. You moved over me like water,
old water I'd swum in for years, knowing where
the bottom fell away, where warmth became a shiver,
then warmth again, you let me weep, you left
your smell all over me as if you'd just walked
naked in our garden, juniper, rosemary, snow's
blue flowers melting on your skin, our bodies
old, now one year older. I swear I won't get used to this,
your cries muffled in my hair, the hurt and no-one-touching
that my mother has to bear; a thousand miles
away from us, a single setting at her table
this first day of her eighty-eighth new year.

MY FATHER, FACE TO FACE

I am afraid to meet my father
in the other world. Afraid
he'll be lonely, sad, and still
I won't be big enough –
my body as I know it gone –
to comfort him.

I failed him – there, I've
said it – coming home
from university for Christmas
and for summer jobs,
thinking I knew more
than him, thinking I was better,
though greeting him face to face
at the door, I insisted our rare
dry kiss was on the lips.

Years later, just before his death,
too sick to walk, he drove me to the bus.
I made myself say, I love you, Dad,
and he replied, I love you too,
and used my name.

We sat in the parking lot,
his big hands on the wheel though
the car was stopped, a late spring
snow stuck to the windows
so we couldn't see out. I wish
I'd known then that his drinking
was a sickness not a sin.

The radio was on to catch the weather;
the names of towns and falling temperatures
saved us from each other. Maybe
when I see him next
there'll be no need for me to try
to take away the shame.

Maybe all the things grief gives us
mean nothing there, and face to face,
we'll feel no more
than wind, than grass, though sometimes
both to me seem full of sorrow.

THE LONGEST NIGHT

The stars go out,
the clouds like clouds
everywhere forget,
but the sky holds all
the heart can give it,
which is less
than light, which is more.

OBSESSION

I think *moth* and the Miller moth
appears. Out of my mind
it sits on the kitchen windowpane
between pieces of smutty wings
I've smashed on the glass.

What would Issa do? He who told
the spiders they had nothing to fear –
he kept house poorly. He was
also wise and Buddhist; knew spiders
do their work quietly, alone.

I've done my best to see
this moth's large extended family
as things of use or beauty,
winter blossoms in an empty house,
fertile clots of earth sprouting legs and wings,
leaving the kind of trail
dirt would leave if it crawled
momentarily up a window
or fell between plates on a white cloth.

I try to think of its feelers as curled
eyelashes on a sweet-faced boy,
as two delicate pubic hairs
a lover might leave on the sheets.

This moth could've been cut
from the wool of Raskolnikov's long coat –
a ragged repentant from another realm
sent to stay the murderer in me.

THE DEAD TWIN

It's best not to know most of us *in utero*
are half a set of twins, the brother or sister dead,
absorbed by the survivor until there's nothing left of it
but a thin-as-paper glyph. Inside my mother
my small familiar curled beside me. I soaked it up,
pressed it like a precious flower into the amnion.
Now I blindly carry it, personal watermark on skin,
stain on the lining of my lung, my way of knowing
what is only mine to know. Is it the root of loneliness?
A second self flickering in the shadow
the brain casts in the skull? After my mother and father,
it was the first to give me life and I took it fast.
Coming out of sleep I sometimes hear the soft underblows
that fall between my heartbeats like a pale unformed
finger tapping from inside, *I am, I am, I am.*

THE DEAD TWIN 2

Is it better, after all, to be the other twin,
the limbless innocent, the dumb? The one
my mother carries like a small greasy
thumbprint on the wall of her old womb.
My life in this world is almost done;
I've cheated, lied, envied my betters,
pinched a child just to hear it cry,
mourned a cat more than my father,
betrayed, betrayed. As Roethke said,
I'd rather eat than pray.
The other one is gentle as a mayfly,
delicately daft, a midge of being,
pure and never tried.
It has no bones, I have holes in mine.
Newt, wren, snow cricket: they nudge me
like a memory, it hurts to look at them.
Light douses the beauty in a lily's throat,
falls across a wrist, turned just so
on a windowsill. All my life I've praised
the moon but it loves best the nearly born,
the little death that won't lie still
until I die.

THE END OF MARRIAGE

When snow is falling it's possible
you'll feel listless. Snow, after all,
smothers everything, street signs, garden
lanterns, the sad hump of the dog buried in the yard
three years ago, what you can and cannot see.
Snow makes you ask, What's the use?
It takes away tomorrow. Every destination
becomes the point of your departure, the word
or moment you knew you had to leave
now heavy with white and cold
like boughs of cedar, bearing down.
There's no end to this lassitude;
the guilt, the good intentions drift
higher than the windowsills, bury the bike
one of you left against the fence all winter.
Outside the house, snow fleeces your head
and shoulders, the toes of your boots.
Backwards, arms spread, you fall into it.
Easy to imagine you've grown wings
marvellous and lit, and as you sink, you fly.

GRIEF RESUMÉ

(A newspaper article collected some of the errors found in cover letters submitted to potential employers. One was "Enclosed is my grief resumé" and another has become the last line of this poem.)

A budgie my brother named Tweety.
Two dogs, both in childhood.
One beagle when I was thirty.
Grandparents before that.
My father, then my mother.
She lived sixteen years alone.
Two cats buried in the garden.
Too many friends.
Once I could count them
on one hand.

I look forward to an interview at your convenience.
Hope to hear from you shorty.

THE FIFTH ELEMENT

The breathy idioms of the wind –
the best translator would be the aspens
if that were their task.

In the house, the woman opens the fridge,
takes out a carton and folds back the top.
Says to her husband, Smell this.

What she means is
it's all over. The expiration date
long passed. Meanwhile

back at the aspens, the leaves
have decided to imitate water.
They do it well, so much so,

if you were blindfolded and led
beneath their boughs, you'd anticipate
mist on your face and a tumble over stones.

How did they learn this?
Living all their lives so far
from any river, in a land of drought.

Maybe it's the wind that's
teaching them, knowing water
as it does, and air and earth and fire.

She wonders why wind
isn't the fifth element.
Did the ancients think of it

as simply air, air
that wouldn't stand still?
Times like this

she wishes
she'd studied Aristotle
so she could better

frame her argument.
Right now all she has is
this feeling about the wind

and what it seems to say to her
as she breathes it in,
quiero, quiero, quiero,

the first verb she learned
on their first vacation
thirty years ago

and the only one
she's kept: *quiero, quiero, quiero,*
I want, I want, I want.

AFTER EDEN

Their first night out, the moon
flowered above them, its scent
the scent of hyacinths when everything
was new, and all night, as before,
a fine pollen drifted down, softened them
from head to toe. Hours before sunrise
they heard the animals pass by, bewildered
and betrayed. Not one stopped to greet them
though their skin ached for a touch of wing, a nuzzle,
the heat from a bigger heart. Night after night
the moon rose higher. It lost its smell,
and they felt something shift inside them:
their minds grew cold. Everything, even the god
who cursed and yelled and drove them out,
became more distant and abstract.

WHAT HOLDS YOU

Swatches of snow on the hills
where the clouds have rested
all afternoon and left their down.

This is what you see at sunset
when the hills turn off their lights,
swan clouds, ghost clouds, suspended
between the dark and nothing

as you are, your parents
and your old friends gone,
long unattended. The sky's
the only childhood thing
that isn't smaller
than you remember it.

At dawn the hills
return, predictable as
the old dog who sleeps
too much, a comfort at least
in their diurnal habits,
the familiar place they occupy
as they circle and lie low

and you don't need
to stand in any doorway
to call them home.

THE DAY MY FRIEND IS DYING

The ocean is as grey
as the back of a heron,
and it's just as still.

Water stares into water,
hunting itself;
a rare snow is falling.

What is silent is more silent.
Beach stones, driftwood,
mallards and mergansers,

two crows on a rock
capped with snow.
They look happy

to be black
in all this grey and white.
This is what it's like

to be alive in the world.
A gull cries out,
catches the updraft

then disappears,
the sky a drift of down.
At this moment

there's no reason
for the crows
to make a sound.

OUR GOOD AND COMMON BONES

Dancing with the Rats

A wood rat dances on the fallen shingle.
Such a spring to his steps, there must be horsehair
underneath. Our rat feet want to join him.

The arborists despair. Billions of books
and so few about trees! Unless all
that paper speaks for itself.

Only the crows look after the wind.
They dive at your head to keep from harm
its airy fledglings high in the poplar leaves.

The man who gave himself to lightning
was afraid of the dark. His wife walks out
in every storm to wave hello.

There is a moon in everything: wineglass,
blue plum, the shine of the old ones
when the night comes down.

The Onion Seller

The nuthatch climbs the spruce upside down
and backwards. See, friends, if you're bored,
there's another way of doing things.

Two bumpy sacks of onions balance
in a curved basket above the wheel.
Everything's round to the onion seller on his bike.

Half-in, half-out of shadow, his black
tail flicking, the cat is of two minds,
both of them indisputably cat.

No rain for weeks on the wheat fields.
The sun bends close with its magnifying glass,
the sky bright as boiled bone.

Surely a horse has brought me here!
I've come so far to meet my lover
and my mouth smells of hay.

Cottonwood

So much cotton from the cottonwood
you can weave enough sheets
for every bed you'll ever lie in.

Brother James shaved his whole head.
It's a nice shape, I tell him, from the good
thoughts he's been having all these years.

The peonies dropped to their knees
in last night's rain. Now they can't get up!
Too much devotion's bad for you.

Old man on a bicycle asks if I want a ride.
He likes my sway, he says. Yesterday
he was that gawky boy who swung from branches.

Think of the blue veins in the cow's udder.
That's the blue the cats dream of
when their whiskers twitch in sleep.

Many Hands Waving

The high clear forehead of the moon
gets you thinking. Why does no one
want a lover as fine as you?

The right kind of weather in the words
and the wheat's as plush as any prayer rug,
in the middle of the field, many hands waving.

Absent-minded, the wind forgets
where it's going. It shifts direction
just when it was at my back, urging me along.

What do the dead undo? A raincloud's zipper,
melons, the stubbornness of roses. Not
the common human losses that undo you.

Wine and music aren't enough.
Leaves in the cornfield rustle and rub together,
the sound of a couple whispering in bed.

Small Mechanics

Morsel of sleek and four trim feet.
It takes so little cheese to catch the mouse.
Is there time for him to taste it?

Under a sky that keeps no secrets,
the field stone hides
what it's holding deep inside.

Why complain about the cold? The badger wants
to test his fur for winter, and your old bones
need dress rehearsals for the fleshless times.

The shadow in the empty barn has blood in it;
the smell of dust and shorn hair settles
on your shoulders like a grandfather's worn coat.

I want a poet who goes outside,
who knows the small mechanics
of the clothespin and the muddy boot.

St. Sebastian

Say you are lonely. There are miseries
the choirs can't sing even in the great cathedrals
that make a slave child of the light.

No matter what, the grass holds on, holds on.
You tug and you fall over, little spears
making St. Sebastians of your hands.

The cat brings in a beetle and lets it go,
brings in a tree frog and lets it go. How soft
and affable her mouth, for all the teeth inside it.

Round shoulders hunched, the moon drinks
at the lakeshore. It drinks its own reflection.
Always pale and thirsty, then, that moon.

A plank bridge over a grassy ditch
where water never flows. Yet in crossing it,
you sense something risked and changed.

Before the Talk Begins

You look into the sunny sky and see your life –
wind herding the clouds so fast, you're drenched
before the five steps to your door.

The Sorrow Bird, the last to stop its singing.
During the yearly bird count, the watchers write:
Name unknown.

Such silence in the white peony,
yet when the petals fall you hear each one,
small breath inhaled, just before the talk begins.

Where do the flies that madden the cows
go at night? Under the leaves, upside down,
blood pooling in their hard heads.

It is the deaf mute who saves the owl feather;
the blind man who saves those cracked rounds
of colour in the painter's tin.

In This, the Hummingbird

Nothing's more devoted than my right foot.
It goes with me everywhere. It loves me more
than Neruda loved his mohair sock.

Bones migrate underground to rest beneath
country churches. They like the creaking of the planks
above, and the day the animals are blessed.

Every mile, a road meets the one you're on,
sometimes a turnoff to a house no light has visited for years.
Still, you think you hear the old dog barking.

Friends, be like Han-shan in the time of T'ang.
When the gift-givers arrived at his mountain,
he yelled, *Thief, thief!* and ran to hide.

In this, the hummingbird resembles us:
he goes for red – crocosmia, geranium,
the rilled roof of the tomcat's mouth.

Common Bones

Bed piled high with books!
Where is my lover? At home in the city
with the garden cats and eleven kinds of bamboo.

Wisdom brings no comfort, only wisdom.
The trouble with God, the poet tells us,
he doesn't know when the soup needs more salt.

On the trail I run through the woods,
an old man comes from the opposite direction.
Boy, you've got a lot of life left in you, he says.

Li Po passed out in apple blossoms, woke up
in snow, the mango birds and children gone.
Was that his wife, that stooped woman singing?

For all our differences, short, tall, blue-eyed,
brown, our mouths used to bitter or sweet,
we have our good and common bones.

Knocking on Different Doors

On the grid your feet become ghost feet,
trail behind you small asthmatic breaths.
Even the children grow old in this dust.

Knocking on wood: the sound of potatoes
dropped into a pail, one by one. Did you know
your digging opens so many doors under the earth?

Winter night, the woman watched three hares
dance in the snow below the moon. Now she's dead:
white hares, white fields, white flesh.

A man who doesn't know how to handle a hoe
shouldn't hold a pen. From the Book of Ecclesiastes,
Do not try to be smart when you do your work.

The lightning wasn't lightning but a flying fox!
How else do you explain the charred bones
of chickens where the storm struck the ground?

What Will Listen

Today the wind has muscle. It pushes me back,
pushes me back, until I fear I'll see my father
building himself behind me, breath by breath.

This constant looking out! Is it the hunter
inside me, or the lonely one?
What different things do they make me see?

New planks in the barn, one wall propped with poles.
Now the horses can come back, *Dolly, Bill,*
and *Greysilk* in fading paint above the stalls.

Mid-November, near the end of the affair,
the aging poet who walks the High Marsh Road
writes, *My curses begin to threaten my whistling.*

In the grass, the bright abacus of water beads
on spiders' webs. How Chinese their measure!
Walk a line, the drops tremble but do not fall.

Someone Must Be Drowning

It's easy to learn how to hold a funeral:
the bluebottle flies, the grieving wind, any number
of pines will tell you. But how to live one day!

The blue of flax creates in you such tenderness
someone must be drowning. If a body washes up,
wrap it in linen and paint a face where a face should be.

Rain falls and falls and doesn't change you
though dry in their burrows, moles
turn into fortune tellers and prophesy the dark.

A breeze ripples the grass, an orchestra
of miniature accordions, buttons made of
bird bones and the C notes of beetle backs.

To clear the air, I've hired mice to separate
the salt and pepper. Can't you hear those
plosive sneezes push away the mist?

All the Lovers Look the Same

An overdose of yellow in canola blossoms
dulls your other senses. In the heart of the field,
hundreds of phones ringing, and you don't hear.

The singer opens the story: *Go to the temple of Anu*
and Ishtar: open the copper chest with the iron locks;
the tablets of lapis lazuli tell the tale.

Today I turn off the tap. Tomorrow I may open it.
That's no way to carry on. I must learn from willows,
from frogs the size of guitar picks that thrum the green.

The same amount of light, but the moon shrinks
as it rises. Imagine the pressure in its skull! Is this why
it forgets so much, and all the lovers look the same?

Someone observing the wings of bats – how they
open and fold – invented fans. Held in the hand,
they create the coolness of caves.

A Cow's Eye

On the grid road the wind blows a hundred years
of travel past your ears: such groaning
in the wood and iron wheels.

The farmer says it's a bad photograph.
Never take a picture of a cow's eye or a man's.
Include the head, the whole head, and the shoulders.

All the gods invisible or fractured, the man makes
a god of his two fists, then pulls on gloves
to keep his holiness soft and bloodless.

A barn owl's face is pale and heart-shaped
and as close to human
as a bird's can get.

You want the poem to be a thing of light
moths can land on, without singeing
their *en pointe* feet.

Holy One

A swarm of dragonflies! So intricate and golden,
surely a watchmaker assembled their parts
to give his children a lighter, leaner sense of time.

The woman could hear the bear chewing her head.
Brother, she said. *Father, Holy One*. Now when the bear
hears her voice in his belly, he stands like a man and dances.

The underside of the cloud that blinds the sun:
the same colour as the inside of the girl's eyelids.
When the light changes, she is changed.

North of here doesn't mean tundra. But the arctic bed
behind the door you'll one day open, the dirty string
you'll pull to bring the cold dark down.

A chickadee lighting on your palm:
hard to believe the soul weighs less than that
and does not sing.

That's All There Was

Wind talks to itself. So does the rain.
Only dust engages you in conversation
and it gets the last word every time.

Rilke calls Cezanne's blues "a thunderstorm," "a listening,"
and mails his wife a letter whose blue he names
"the clear breathing of being alone."

A wave, a whiter wave, a loss of words
at high tide and at low. The way of water and the moon:
they draw us close to what we can't get close to.

Long-billed curlew, someone's son, friends
who paid with coins to cross the terrible river
where Adam waits to take away their names.

Snow falls the way it fell in childhood, a soft sigh
then a hush. Hard to find a meaning in it –
that's all there was.

The Grasshopper's Task

A woman falls in the yard. The wash keeps flapping
on the line. A week later her husband takes it in,
but the frayed white slip – he leaves hanging.

How the earth aches for its losses! Some days
you feel it in your feet and need to thicken
the leather in your boots to keep on walking.

It's the grasshopper's task to eat everything
getting in its way. What if we did that?
How full we'd be of envy!

Potatoes: more like us than any other vegetable.
In the root cellar their long pale arms
reach for one another in the dark.

Is it possible for an hour, maybe less than that,
to see things clearly? Your brow, for instance,
a cathedral dome full of light.

Prophecy of Birds

A snake's tongue licks your ears.
Now you understand at last
the prophecy of birds.

My friend shovelled the walk
wearing the gloves of her dead husband,
her hands, his hands, clearing the snow.

Throat's hollow, between the collar bones,
mine's deep enough to hold a worry stone,
a knot to hitch the wind.

A nunnery of snails, each in its hard
brown habit, making thin traceries of lace
from winter lettuce.

My mother washed me in water
rats had drowned in. To make me brave,
she said, but I wonder to this day.

Telling the Story Backwards
(after Robert Hass)

The first to return was the ivory-billed woodpecker
in the mangrove swamps, solitary and shy.
Soon no one could believe their multitude and noise.
Farther south, in Buenos Aires, a tiger stepped
brilliant and dangerous from a blind man's dream.
In colder climes what manifested next were prairie grizzly,
black-footed ferret, dusky seaside sparrow, so delicate
the bird seemed made of mist. Then the clouds
let go their nets, wrens and warblers tumbled
from the sky, thrushes, orioles, finches beyond number.
The speech of humans changed with that galaxy of sound
larking the dawn. In the cities, people began to disappear,
wind blustered in the boardrooms, rain rode down
the elevator shafts. Words vanished like belugas in the past:
toxins, for instance, *feed lot, Weyerhaeuser, hydro dam,*
    Monsanto.
Instead, exclamation marks and sightings riffed off the page:
Three-toed sloths! in an L.A. parking lot. *Snow leopards!*
Bumblebees the size of damsel plums, Atlantic cod,
cohoe, cohoe! Those lucky to be left surmised
the population lost had been pulled into the sea. In water's
silver flash and boil, mistaken for a shoal of herring,
are humans, more or less, becoming
what they once had been.

Small Courtesies

My friend with the red truck and the shovel
stops up the road to break the ice on the dugout.
When I head back, he's pulled into a yard
in front of me, the house closed up but a small corral
holds a brown horse and a blue. He climbs
the fence and hugs them as I pass, one
after the other, his arms around their necks,
his face buried in the winter thickness of their hair.
A privacy I'm sure I wasn't meant to see.

I've used "friend" with no rights to it.
We just happen to meet around
the same time every morning, me climbing
the road for exercise, him out to break the ice
and feed his cattle, splitting a round of hay
into flays he spreads upon the frozen ground.
Beyond these chores, I wonder what his life is like.

The third day I walked past, he asked me,
"Aren't you wearing yourself out, climbin' this hill?"
How carefully he figures out a way to discover
who I am and what I'm doing here, his question
impersonal enough, an opening as big or small
as I want to make it. A week went by before he asked,
"How many running shoes you gonna use up?"
and I let him know I'm here only for the month,
then back to the city, "Victoria," I said, "B.C."
He's never left the ranch his granddad started.
My mother in her eighties, I told him, still lives
in Swift Current where I grew up

and grows enough potatoes to last the winter.
Ignorant of the small courtesies required, I asked
if I could give his horses a carrot next time I went by.
"Sure – if they'll eat it."

He's around fifty, I'd guess, his round face
made rounder by a cap with ear flaps.
Lots of sun-lines and foxing from the wind.
"How about this weather?" I said yesterday.
"Love it," he said, and told me not to worry
about the lack of snow. A wet May filled the creeks.
Sure of our rhythms now, I say, "See ya tomorrow."

There's something reassuring in our simple talk,
our clockwork that isn't based on clocks. It has to do
with the sun being high enough for us to do our tasks,
with his need to open water early for the cattle,
my need to walk. Soon it will be over and
I'll be back at work, teaching poetic theory
in a class, noting meetings in a day book.

I don't know if he could feel me watching
when he climbed the fence
and hugged his horses. I like to think
it wouldn't have bothered him. From the road
I saw his hefty body in its overalls press
against the warmth, me close enough to see
their breaths become one cloud, one weather,
my friend with the red truck and the shovel,
the brown horse and the blue.

Midnight Watch

(after Thomas Hardy's "The Oxen")

At midnight on Christmas Eve, it is said,
the animals in the barn will kneel:
the grey horse with spotted haunches,
the two pygmy goats on their mountain of bales,
the old duck with one lame foot, and all the dogs
you've ever known, who'll become this night
one dog – thick, black coat and a blaze down his nose;
in the barn, it is said, the animals will kneel.

What you need is faith, something you've had
little of all your life. What you need is
the stubborn, singular belief
that if you pull on your coat and boots
and walk to the barn in the steady rain or snow,
if you drag the chopping block to the window
and peer inside, the animals will be on their knees,
their breath a wreath of fog around their heads.

Only the cat will sit on the straw outside their circle,
one ear turned to the others, one toward you,
as if she's on watch, as if she's meant to give a warning.
Or perhaps she'll be there, halfway between
the animals and you, so you won't feel unblessed
in your strange human skin, you won't feel alone,
peering into a darkness you can't see through,
somewhere a star coldly shining.

Extreme Creation

The hummingbird – fierce
miniature flower, its long stamen
hardened to a beak. He cut it
from its stem, fastened
tiny feet, and let it fly.

This happened
on the last day in the hour
set aside so he could look
at everything he'd done and
change his mind,

turn blossoms into birds and vice versa,
dapple, split, ravish, shirr
the million things he'd made,
(deepening the dip
behind a woman's clavicles, painting
red stripes on the turtle's long cheeks)

add outrageous beauty and its opposite:
the shit-brown
slime of wood slugs

to which he affixed,
to mix it up,
more delicate than newborn fingers,
two soft horns
touched with the tip of his tongue
to make them shine.

A New Religion
(after Philip Larkin's "Water")

If I were called in
        to construct a new religion
I should make use of cats.

Several would have fur
between their toes – Maine coons perhaps –
so they could re-enact the miracle
        and walk on snow
without falling through.

In schools of theology
        cats would teach
prayers of purring, priests-in-training
laying hands on one another's bellies,
        feeling at last
the warm wheels of devotion
whirring inside their flesh.

In every parish
there'd be a jersey cow
grazing among the graves;
        churches would be praised
for mouse-infested vestries,
and the sermons too often
would tell the story of Jesus
        never running out of fish.

All services would be held
after sunset, in candlelight,
                those strange eyes staring
through the dark
past the pews, the altars, seeing
what the preachers and their congregations
        long to see.

Best would be the cats' constant
                comings and goings –
doors in every place of worship
opened, then shut; opened, then shut –
reminding the doubters, the righteous,
        and the less-than-holy
of the soul's
                restless journeys
away from and back to the world.

Dostoevsky

He was a man unconvinced by pancakes.
He said that, as she licked the syrup off her fingertips.
Funny, it happened all the time. Though she never touched
the pancakes, syrup travelled up her fork and made
her fingers stick. She wondered if the rich ate this victual
with thin white gloves a maid would pull off after.
She would have called this man a boy but she was trying
not to see others from the perspective of her longevity.
She'd grown old since her mother died two years ago.
Was that common? You age instantly even as a child
upon your mother's death? Take on the look of children
in those old Italian paintings, stern adult heads stuck on
little bodies padded with velvets and brocade.
The man uninspired by pancakes had the face of a monk.
A monk had told him that and it made him wonder
if he should join the order. He needed a letter of reference
from an employer but he was out of work, merely
a doctoral student on a grant. She noticed he had nice ankles.
They would show beneath a robe. What did it mean
to look like a monk? The ones she knew were old, shrunken
to the size of a child, their skin transparent. When they
    bathed,
could you see their hearts breaking through, by the tub
undershirts tacky with blood? She wondered if this aspirant
knew Dostoevsky's *So much grief, and then pancakes after.*
Of course he did. They all read the Russians now
and deconstructed them. Break down a pancake
and it wasn't much: flour, baking powder, an egg.
What had she forgotten? There must be sugar, at least half
    a cup.
There must be salt. So much grief would add the tears.

Bestiary for Fox and Owl

There's a red fox by the Frenchman River
with an owl in his mouth. He could have
stepped on narrow paws from the illuminated
margins of an ancient book, strange creature,
sharp-nosed and furred with a grey wing
on either side of his tapered head.
The illustrator, once a farm boy,
would have called him *Fox-owl*, or less earthy,
tempted by Latin and myth, *Vulpes psychopomp*,
bearing the owl's big-eyed soul to the river's other shore.
It's a great-horned, one of the smaller but not lesser
gods, as the fox is, of the hills and grasses.

Yesterday my husband called me
from my reading, said he had a surprise –
on its belly on the kitchen table was this owl,
wings spread, blood pooling around
its crushed curved head. He'd found it on
the highway and brought it home.
Even motionless, left wing out of joint,
it filled the kitchen with a presence
we couldn't name. *Poor dead
thing*, I said, *poor beautiful thing*,
and stroked its feathers, felt the sharpness
of its claws, the hard muscles in its catlike
thighs, bigger than we would have guessed,
the downy whisper of its belly. We took it
to the riverbank behind the house
and released it to the air as if it were
an injured bird we'd healed. It fell into
the deeper hush of snow and yellow grasses.

Now there's nothing left but tracks, a row
of paw prints with the brush of wings on either side,
and even though we know there is a fox, owl
in his mouth, it's easy to see the opposite:
an owl dropping down to catch a fox,
its wings brushing the snow, then lifting,
rowing across the blue, fox pulled tight
against the feathered chest, red head under the owl's chin,

the illustrator now working fast by candlelight
to get it right before it's only something
he's made up, four red legs dangling like a crow's
about to land, his brush spelling
what he can almost see: a new way of being
hammering the air, all the birds and animals
for miles pausing in their tasks
as a creature half-alive, more extraordinary
than any angel, more terrible and true,
flies the upper margins of the sky.

Early Morning, November 11, 2009

At first it was merely mist,
as if I were walking under clothesline
after clothesline pinned with scarves.

Then rain needled me to the cold.
I raised my face to its falling,
my feet skidding on the yellow

slime of leaves. I raised my face
so I'd feel the sharp and wet of it.
This was all I could think to do

past the middle of my life, a woman
with a warm house waiting, my walk
almost done –

how small a link, how inadequate:
rain on my aging face, my
open mouth clear of mud.

Not Enough to Call It Murder

Five crows plunging and rising
above the field, calling out,
one always slightly behind, not
the same crow, they're taking turns,
the back-rider glancing over its wings
at what gets lost in so much
noise and scatter.

Black ash of the future, the four in front
head toward me. Nothing I can do
but watch them coming, so cocky
in their crow-ness I know they've never
had another life. Now they're right above,

Old Testament of matter, quoting Job.
In their shadows I feel odd, as if
I've just become someone's memory,
perhaps the crow who lags behind,
his eye on me, his slow wings beating.

Garden, Night, Listening

Night spills its darkness into the sky.
The two cats at my feet hear what I cannot –
the silence and not silence of its many wings –
even when I shake my head so the bones
start their shift, hammers and anvils
in the small factories of the inner ears,
stirrups that carry me away from my body's
sitting still. Deeper into the garden, my lover
walks in a blue-black robe. Beyond my seeing,
a match scrapes on its ribbon of grit; suddenly
his face, the flare of it, briefly blessed.
At the pond one of the cats hunches and drinks,
the slap of his tongue, a pulse quickening the dark.
On its own the pond never makes a sound.
Its silence is the silence of water, listening.

Finally

The word *love* means someone takes you
in your old clothes, your face too bare, too open,
when someone fastens the buttons on your coat
as if you've fallen back through sixty years to be
a child again, when someone takes you onto the path
holding you by the arm, your feet not knowing what
they used to know, your feet in rubber boots stumbling,
blind to roots and stones, when someone takes you
to the ocean, the water also in the air raining down
its saltless weeping. The word *love* means someone
takes you to the rocks, rain too heavy for the gulls
to lift, three bobbing like windless boats, all sails
and heartbeat, love leaves you there, no words
for it now, you and the gulls and the ocean
that moves as far away from you as it can go.

My Last Erotic Poem

Who wants to hear about
two old farts getting it on
in the back seat of a Buick,
in the garden shed among vermiculite,
in the kitchen where we should be drinking
ovaltine and saying no? Who wants to hear
about twenty-six years of screwing,
our once-not-unattractive flesh
now loose as unbaked pizza dough
hanging between two hands before it's tossed?

Who wants to hear about two old lovers
slapping together like water hitting mud,
hair where there shouldn't be
and little where there should,
my bunioned foot sliding
up your bony calf, your calloused hands
sinking in the quickslide of my belly,
our faithless bums crepey, collapsed?

We have to wear our glasses to see down there!

When you whisper what you want I can't hear,
but do it anyway, and somehow get it right. Face it,
some nights we'd rather eat a Häagen-Dazs ice cream bar
or watch a movie starring Nick Nolte who looks worse than us.
Some nights we'd rather stroke the cats.

Who wants to know when we get it going
we're revved up, like the first time – honest –

like the first time, if only we could remember it,
our old bodies doing what you know
bodies do, worn and beautiful and shameless.

Grocery List

I walked into the sea on the way to buy groceries.
Bored I was with the shouting of the shelves,
the metal cart and its stubborn rubber wheels,
bored with the sureness of my feet hitting the level,
the hard polished floor. The sea rose around me
cold and invasive, tugging at my skirt and jacket,
my soft Italian shoes. By the time I reached
the meat aisle, I was doing the breaststroke,
the flutter kick, the dead man's float, behind me
my feet – voracious bottomfeeders,
each toe a sucking mouth. How this new life
suited them! Something thick and noseless
bumped against my calves. I tried to recall
what it was I needed. Shallots, I said out loud,
red potatoes, Shredded Wheat.
The shoppers in the aisles were strangely dry
and watching. The list from my pocket –
suddenly so vital – drifted out of reach.
There were things I knew I was forgetting.
Love? I said. Dijon, Heartache? Day-old bread?

Outside Eden

She began to keen –
he'd never heard anything like it –
and pull her hair.

Nothing had died yet.
Nothing had been born.
He moved away from her.

After a week she stopped,
and they slept together
to keep warm.

Now the sound came out
only when they mated.
It frightened him.

For this, if he'd been asked,
though he'd come up with
eel, ibis, hippopotamus,

he couldn't have found
a name.

Taking the Measure

The belly's post-menopausal slouch,
under each bicep the swag of a fleshy wing,
dollops of fat above my bra below my armpits
flap and make smacking noises when I run. Long as
the face of a foal, my breasts meander, my cheeks
droop. Naked, I look in mirrors only on the sly
and never try the ones in hotel bathrooms. Some claim
wisdom but my mind sags, too. *Au revoir*
to high-school French and long division, to the seven
kinds of ambiguity, the common names of flowers,
and Shakespeare learned by heart. To be has taken over
not to be. So be it. For that I'm grateful.
I and my lover of long duration still turn to each other
in the night and in the morning and in the fierce-eyed
glare of afternoon. The years, he says, have made me
elemental. I taste more and more like salt.

The Bad Poem

No matter what the quality of the crystal,
the silverware you've laid on the linen cloth,
this is the kind of poem
that farts at the dinner table. The other guests,
people you'd hoped would become friends,
pretend they don't hear. You wonder if
they're the type who don't listen to poems
at the best of times, even when they rhyme
and smell of flowers. You're about to say
you don't know who invited this one,
it must've been your husband, your teenaged son,
but then it farts again, and everyone falls quiet.

It would like to disown you, too, you know,
it would like to have come from someone else,
Bukowski, Purdy perhaps, or Dorothy Parker
with runs in her stockings and hair of smoke.

Why doesn't someone laugh?
This is your chance to introduce
one of your nicer poems, in the kitchen now,
icing the carrot cake with the right amount of
sweetness and cream cheese, but you feel a crankiness
fluttering inside you like a cloth-eating moth.
If the poem were a dog, you wonder, would you
be so embarrassed? An old family dog under the table,
licking the lotion off a woman's calves, she talking
across the bowls of *oso buco* as if there were
no fat tongue sliding from her ankle to her knee.

It could be worse, you think.
You took a risk with the menu – the guests
could've been vegans for all you knew
and wept for hours over the bones and marrow.
It could be you suffering from flatulence,
less in control of the sounds your body makes
than you used to be, and the dog,
for fifteen years more smelly and more loyal
than anything you've ever written,
could be under the table, right now, wetly humping
the trousered leg of the shyest person in the room.

Needles

His house was full of needles,
a few in plain sight, others
hidden between books or under
cushions, and one I found
on the floor of my car he'd borrowed,
lying there beside a Mars Bar wrapper,
harmless, I suppose, though it made me cringe.
I threw it out and said nothing to him,
knowing he'd be ashamed.
Such a gentleman he was no matter
what his state, and loyal to his friends.

Now he's gone, I watch his wife in their house
with a different kind of needle in her hand.
The tip blunt, a dropper draws milk from a cup
to feed the runt of the litter. She hadn't noticed
how small the kitten was
until she caught the mother with it in her mouth,
heading out the door.

Watching the kitten pull on plastic
I wonder what's the use but I don't say so.
The other four, I know, will be hard enough
to give away. Maybe since her husband left
she needs something close to dying
she can hold in her hand, some
small thing sucking from a needle
that will make it live.

Patience

Most beautiful –
          the Chinese cricket cage
without a cricket.

Just a sadness
          whittled to a thinness
that fits inside:

now you must begin
          to teach it
how to sing.

Missing

From every book, the word flies out
from whatever story held it.
You wonder where it goes,
if it will stay outside all winter without harm.

For weeks you leave strands of wool
on branches; you put out food: a tasty
adjective, a verb that dithers like an insect.

You never see it clearly but sometimes
you glimpse the wit of its wings
as they dip and dive above the water.

Sentences throw out their nets but
it cuts right through them. You leave
a window open but it won't fly in.

You're not sure what word it is.
You try the big ones you'd like to say
goodbye to – *guilt, grief, envy, death,*
but page after page they're still there.

It must be a lighter word,
perhaps a silly one,
for it to fly away without
a note of consequence, for it to

leave behind a space so small
it's goes unnoticed, unremarked
in all the learnèd journals.

Are you the only one who feels
a lack of something
in every book you read,
in every truth you try to tell?

Reader

The cat licks
one of your eyelids,
then the other.

The way you lick
a finger
to turn a page.

The Ambiguity of Clouds

Never mind, the clouds say
as they drift above you. Never mind.
When you first heard them
as a child, you thought they meant

all would be fine
if you didn't obsess, if you didn't
let things fester.

Time has taught you another
meaning; death has taught you,
loneliness has taught you.
It's never the mind

that gets you close to beauty,
the first and last of things,
or any of the wisdoms you long to know.

It has something to do with horses,
the warm smell of your lover's neck
where it meets the shoulder,
the silence of aspen groves
when the wind falls still.

Never mind, never mind.
Is it possible the clouds say that,
mindless as they are? All
body, if you can call them that,
cumulative and ephemeral,
fish bones,

a lung bleached of blood,
an inky brain, not thinking.

P. K.

She saw two moons in the prairie sky.
As a girl, when asked if she were cursed
with seeing double, she replied,
Oh, no. If I were, then I'd see four.

In countries with no cold,
snow from her childhood
fell circular and soft
in the glass globe of her inner eye,
dressing the blossoms as if they were brides.

Her only child was the child she dreamed
and folded in a box like a scarf
woven out of rain. You could say
she neglected God and his angels,
though the invisible made sense
in all her senses. Heaven she found

in the gaze of a glorious macaw
with the face of Groucho Marx,
and once, with her calm uncanny eye,
as a marmoset in a rage sunk its teeth
in the flesh just above her wrist,
she noticed its fingers
were the stems of violets.

In a poem, at the moment of death,
the poet asked, *What is the correct procedure?*
Cut the umbilicus, they said.

Now she has cut it and risen from the page.
Beneath her, the Earth is the size of a plum
and the blue of a plum when it is ripe with morning.
Is the body still a body, she wonders,
if it is drifting so high? How, then, to prepare it?
Wash it in sacred water is her own reply.
Dress it in silk for the wedding.

Summerfallow

I'd thought the bare field
not as beautiful as the others
lit with canola or burnished
with the old bronze of barley
but it's not just snowflakes
that are unrepeated. Each clod of earth
is different from the next, casts its own
clotted shadow, longer in the evening
like the poplar's or the beautiful woman's
as she walks down the road into the stilted
solitude of herself. Tonight I lie down in it,
this dirt sea where unseen boats are moored.
I sink a little like an old grave; my bones come
back to me as if they've been somewhere
I couldn't travel. Sometimes the spirit of all
troubled and untroubled things must be heavy,
so the body knows it's there.

The New Day

Over the eastern farmlands and into the city
light spills unimpeded. Now you can go
into the dark that lives inside you.

Even flies have a mother,
a hard-won grief.

Someone has taught them
to wash and wash their faces
until they shine.